A Very Musician

Written by
Cath Jones

Illustrated by
James Hearne

Ransom

Charlene's teacher looked sternly at the children.

"We have a special musician visiting today. Be sure to sit still and do as she says."

"My name is Zander," said the musician.
"This is my glockenspiel and this is my special,
magic, music machine. Now, are you ready for
some magic music?"

Charlene gazed at the musician's funny hat and
cloak. She couldn't wait for the music to start.

Zander tapped the glockenspiel with some beaters and the room filled with sound.

It made Charlene feel calm and very happy.

"This is my special sound bucket," Zander said. "Can you fill it with sound?"

How odd, thought Charlene, but she whooped into the bucket.

"Fantastic!" shrieked the musician.

"I want this section of the room to cluck like chickens," Zander said.

Lots of children clucked.

"And I want this section of the room to quack like ducks."

The special bucket captured all the clucking and quacking.

Charlene took the bucket back to the musician. She could hardly lift it, which was odd, as sounds aren't heavy. (Or are they?)

Zander went into the school garden with the children. She tipped up the bucket and poured the sounds into the magic machine.

"Press this button," she said.

Charlene pressed the button.

The magic music machine shook and whirred and beeped. A splodge of sound drifted out of the machine and floated into the school kitchen.

POP! The splodge of sound burst.

Then the cooks stopped cooking, as Zander tapped out a beat on the glockenspiel.

Then they started to bash their pans in time to the beat. They made up a fish finger song and sang it very loudly!

The cooks kept on singing, and now they began to dance as they cooked.

Soon, wonderful smells drifted out through the windows. They were the best smells Charlene had ever smelled.

Zander added the cooks' songs to her music machine.

A bit later, Charlene and the children sat down for lunch with Mr Jones, their teacher.

Lunch smelled wonderful!

While everyone was eating, the musician played her glockenspiel.

Mr Jones couldn't stop eating!

Zander winked at Charlene.

"Burp!" A splodge of sound burst from Mr Jones' mouth. Zander caught it in her magic bucket and tipped it into her machine.

"Thank you for all the sounds," she sang. Then she did a little dance as she left the school …

… leaving behind lots of happy, well-fed children!